CANADA THROUGH THE DECADES
THE 1980s

Janice Parker

Weigl

CALGARY

www.weigl.com

Published by Weigl Educational Publishers Limited
6325 - 10 Street SE
Calgary, Alberta, Canada
T2H 2Z9
Web site: http://www.weigl.com
Copyright © 2000 WEIGL EDUCATIONAL PUBLISHERS LIMITED

Canadian Cataloguing in Publication Data

Parker, Janice.
 The 1980s

 (Canada through the decades)
 ISBN 1-896990-40-1

 1. Canada—History—1963—Juvenile literature.* I. Title II. Series.
FC630.P37 1999   j971.064'6   C99-910852-2
F1034.2.P34 1999

Printed and bound in Canada
1 2 3 4 5 6 7 8 9 0   03 02 01 00 99

Editor
Leslie Strudwick
Design
Warren Clark
Copy Editor
Rennay Craats
Layout
Lucinda Cage

Photograph Credits

Every reasonable effort has been made to trace ownership and to obtain permission to reprint
copyright material. The publishers would be pleased to have any errors or omissions brought to
their attention so that they may be corrected in subsequent printings

Archive Photos: pages 16T, 16B, 17T, 18T, 19 T, 27 ML, 34 BL, 38 B, 39 BM, 40 MR; Bruce
Allen Talent: page 38 TM; Thies Bogner: page 25R; CBC Still Photo Collection: pages 13 T, 13
BL; Canadian Space Agency: page 26 TM; City of Calgary Archives: pages 29T, 29B; Corel
Corporation: pages 40 BM, 43 ML; CP Picture Archive: pages 21 BL, 36, 37, 43 BR; Rennay
Craats: pages 10 T, 27 T; Pierre de Mentionner: National Photography Collection: page 23B;
Edmonton Journal: pages 9 T, 28 T, 30 B; Epitome Pictures: page 10 B; Equesport Canada (Jayne
Huddleston): page 30 TL; Forrest Andersen Agencies: page 28 MR; Globe Photos: pages 12 B,
13 MR, 35 M; Hockey Hall of Fame: page 31 M (Miles Nadal); Kristen Higgins: pages 14 MR,
15T, 15B, 34 ML, 41 M; House of Commons: page 23 T; Kids Can Press: page 24 BL; *Leader
Post*: pages 8 T, 42 T; Sorcha McGinnis: page 35 TL; Audra McIntyre: page 35 BM; *Montreal
Gazette*: page 20 MR; MuchMusic: page 39 MR; Robert Munsch: page 24 T; National Archives
of Canada: pages 20 TM, 21 T, 22 T, 23 MR, 25 B; National Film Board of Canada: page 41 TR;
National Research Council: page 26 MR; NASA: page 9 B; Pach Bros, NY: page 19 BL;
PetroCanada: page 33 ML; Photofest: page 34 TR, 34 BR; Ken Read: page 31 TR; Saskatchewan
Archives Board: page 33 M; Science World Vancouver: page 11 ML; Second City: page 11 T;
Sullivan Entertainment: page 12 T; *The Telegram*: page 8 B; Lap-Chee Tsui: page 26 BL; Barbara
Turner: page 25 TL; West Edmonton Mall: page 14 TL.

CANADA THE 1980s Contents

Introduction

The Race for Nuclear Power

From Preppie to Grunge

Space Shuttle Explodes

The Montreal Massacre

Expo 86 "World in Motion— World in Touch"

The Magic of Michael J. Fox

Exxon Disaster

The AIDS Crisis

Tears Are Not Enough

World Shocked by Tiananmen Square

We learn about current events by reading newspapers and listening to news programs on television and the radio. *Canada Through the Decades: The 1980s* takes a look at some of the many news headlines that affected Canada during the decade. Many events affected Canada and Canadians, far too many to feature in this one book. However, we have chosen a variety of stories that affected Canada in different ways. The **Constitution** Act, for example, had an impact on all citizens. Other stories were chosen because they were common experiences. Most Canadians felt sadness when disasters happened in Canada or elsewhere in the world. All of these stories affected Canadians in some way. By learning about what happened during the eighties, you will learn about and better understand Canada's history.

Most stories in Canada never make newspaper headlines.

The Fall of the Berlin Wall

The Quebec Referendum

Royal Wedding

The Marathon of Hope

Tornado Terror

Recession Hits Canada

The Amazing Oilers

SCTV Success

The Madonna Style

These are events that happen in the lives of Canadians every day. Every Canadian has a story to tell. These experiences are also an important part of Canada. After reading this book, you may have some of your own ideas of what other stories it could have contained. Do you know of any events in the 1980s that were important to Canada?

You may have more questions about some of the events that you read about. What happened afterward? Why did it happen? You may want to find out more information on your own. Do some research and see if you can find out more about a story that interests you. Look in encyclopedias and books at the library. Search old newspapers and magazines. The Internet may also be a good source of information. Remember that Canadian history is made up of all of the events that happened throughout time.

1980

Robert Munsch makes himself known to Canadian readers through a royal ambassador. Page 24 gives you more information.

1980

Canadians get caught up with a cube. In 1980, **millions of multi-coloured cubes** are sold. Turn to page 14 for more information about Professor Rubik's successful puzzle.

1981

Canada lends a hand to **space investigation**—actually, it lends an arm. How? Page 26 offers an explanation.

1982

In 1982, Canada officially becomes an **independent** country from Britain. Turn to page 21 to read more.

1982

If you write it, they will read. And read they do. *Shoeless Joe*, W.P. Kinsella's smash **baseball novel**, inspires Kevin Costner to dream. Page 25 tells you how.

1983

The adoption rate skyrockets, especially around Christmas. For more about ten-year-old parents and **sold-out toy** stores, turn to page 15.

1983

Canadians are being told to **"Take Off"** by a couple of hosers, and they think it is funny. Find out more about Bob and Doug on page 11.

1983

Life is so bright for this singer, he has to wear his "Sunglasses at Night." To learn more about this **"Hart-throb"** who ruled 1983, turn to page 38.

1984

The Progressive Conservative party progresses all the way to the prime minister's office. For additional information about its fearless leader and the **nine-year rule**, turn to page 22.

1984

A couple of Canadians accidentally invent a **blockbuster board game**. And there is nothing trivial about that! There are more details on page 10.

1984

In 1984, there is something strange in the neighbourhood. But Canadian Dan Ackroyd knows **who to call**. To read more about *Ghostbusters* turning blockbuster, turn to page 13.

1984

In 1984, it becomes possible to sit at home and watch **music videos** twenty-four hours a day. To learn more about the nation's music station, turn to page 39.

1984

Bryan Adams's tears may not have been enough, but his song is. Turn to page 38 to learn more about **"Northern Lights"** and Live Aid.

1985

A **fiery redhead** takes over Canadian television in 1985. To discover more about Green Gables, see page 12.

1985

With grit and determination and several sets of tires, **Rick Hansen** makes a real difference for people with disabilities. Turn to page 28 to see how this hero helps others.

1985

Residents of Barrie understand how Dorothy and Toto felt. **A tornado** hits the area, causing millions of dollars in damage and claiming several lives. Page 9 has details about deadly weather.

1986

Vancouver wows the world with a **first-rate exhibit**. Page 11 has all the details about Expo 86.

1986

A **radioactive leak** in a Ukrainian nuclear power plant devastates the environment as well as the citizens. People are forced to leave their homes, and some became very ill from contact with radiation. Turn to page 16 to learn more about this nuclear disaster.

1987

The much-talked-about **Meech Lake Accord** fails. Find out why the premiers cannot all sign on the dotted line on page 21.

1987

Canadians go loonie over a **new coin** in 1987. Read more about the crazy currency on page 32.

1987

Nearly 200 Sikhs are **dropped off a boat** and they swim to shore in search of a new life. Turn to page 36 to find out what happened next.

1987

In 1987, the stock **market drops**, and so do people's jaws. Investors watch as they lose a huge amount of money, all within the span of a business day. Read more about the crash on page 32.

1988

A **new disease** terrifies Canada and the world. Health officials estimate that 1,644 Canadians have the disease, and another 30,000 are infected. Learn more about AIDS on page 40.

1988

The **Olympic spirit** takes over Calgary in 1988. Page 29 has more about the athletes, the volunteers, and how the torch reached McMahon Stadium.

1989

Canadians across the country hold vigils every **December 6** since the 1989 tragedy. Discover what happened by turning to page 8.

1989

The border between Canada and the United States is free for **trade in 1989**. But many would sooner trade it in for the old way. Find out why on page 42.

1989

The **wall comes tumbling down** in 1989, uniting a split country in the process. Read about the details on page 17.

1989

Emergency crews try to clean up the mess an oil tanker left behind in 1989. There is more about how an **oil spill** devastates the Alaskan environment on page 19.

The Montreal Massacre

Marc Lepine, twenty-five years old, was angry that he had not been accepted into the École Polytechnique in Montreal. On December 6, 1989, Lepine entered the school armed with weapons. He wandered through the school, shooting and killing fourteen young women and injuring thirteen other people. No one tried to stop him. Then Lepine shot and killed himself. The women Lepine killed had mostly been engineering students. They were all between the ages of twenty-one and twenty-eight years old. Lepine had been a troubled young man who blamed

▌ Memorial services are held across Canada every year on December 6 to remember the fourteen women that were killed in the massacre.

women for ruining his life.

The crime shocked all of Canada. It was the worst mass murder in Canadian history. Many Canadians thought it was an example of anti-female

feelings held by many men around the country. Many others felt it showed that Canada should have stricter gun laws. Lepine had been able to easily purchase a semi-automatic rifle and other weapons.

The federal government has proclaimed December 6 as a National Day of Remembrance and Action on Violence Against Women.

Air Disasters

In June 1985, a man booked seats on two different flights leaving Vancouver. The man did not board either plane, but he placed luggage on both. The man was a terrorist. One piece of

luggage exploded in an airport in Japan, killing two people. The other piece of luggage that contained a bomb was on Air India Flight 182. This plane exploded in the air off the coast of Ireland. The crash was the third worst in history. All 329

people on the plane died. Of these, 280 were Canadian. After the crash, airport security was improved around the world.

The same year there was another plane crash that affected Canada. A plane carrying American soldiers crashed after taking off over Gander, Newfoundland. All 256 people on the plane died. This was the worst air crash that had ever happened over Canadian land. Officials believed the crash was caused by problems with the plane, not by human error.

▌ Many of the plane crashes during the 1980s were due to terrorism. However, the one near Gander, Newfoundland, was likely caused by technical problems.

THE CHALLENGER

Millions of people around the world watched as the space shuttle Challenger prepared to takeoff in January 1986. Space flights always fascinate people, but this one was a little different. Usually, only astronauts and other scientists went into space. On the Challenger was the first private citizen ever to fly into space—Christa McAuliffe. Christa was a high-school social studies teacher from New Hampshire. She was married and had two young children.

All of the students and teachers of Concord High School gathered in the auditorium to watch the shuttle takeoff on television. Christa was a popular teacher. The students were proud that she was chosen to fly into space.

Soon after the Challenger took off, disaster struck. The space shuttle exploded, killing all seven crew members. It was the worst accident in the history of space travel. People around the world mourned the loss of the crew. They were honoured as heroes in the United States.

▥ This tornado swept through Edmonton on July 31, 1987.

Deadly Weather

Weather can sometimes destroy property and kill Canadians. In 1985, a terrible tornado hit Barrie, Ontario. The storm completely destroyed about 300 homes and killed eight people. Thousands of other people were left homeless from the damages. Two years later, a tornado struck Edmonton, Alberta. Homes and other buildings were demolished. A trailer park was the worst hit. Twenty-seven people, most of whom lived in the trailer park, were killed. The storm caused more than $250 million in damages.

Plan for Tomorrow ... Today

During the 1980s, the Canadian government decided to get serious about planning for disasters and other emergencies. In 1981, the government created the Emergency Planning Order, which was to review and improve plans for dealing with disasters. The government also started a program to teach Canadians what to do in case of an emergency. The slogan for this program was "Plan for Tomorrow ... Today." The order was replaced in 1988 by the Emergency Preparedness Act. This new law stated what Canada's role and responsibility was in local, national, and international disasters. The government set up offices in each of the provincial capitals in order to be accessible in case of a disaster. It helped provinces and territories pay for damage done when disasters struck, and it also helped to identify possible emergency situations.

▥ Christa McAuliffe hoped that by going on the shuttle as a person who was not a "space specialist," she would inspire students to learn more about space exploration.

Trivial Pursuit

In 1979, Canadians Scott Abbott and Chris Haney had an argument over who was a better Scrabble player. This challenge over trivia led to the creation of the board game Trivial Pursuit. The two men made the first game out of cardboard. The questions were written on pieces of paper. With two other partners, they scoured library books looking for trivia questions and answers. The four men raised enough money to make several hundred copies of the game.

In 1982, the creators took their game to the International Toy Fair in New York. They only sold a few hundred copies of Trivial Pursuit. Hoping to receive recognition, they decided to send copies to celebrities. Talk show host Johnny Carson mentioned Trivial Pursuit on his late-night talk show. As people began to learn about the game, it became more popular. By the end of 1984, the game had sold over 20 million copies around the world.

▦ By 1999, Trivial Pursuit was being sold in thirty-two countries and in eighteen languages.

"It took us forty-five minutes to design the game and three months to figure out the scoring."

Scott Abbott

TELEVISION

▦ Degrassi is part of the name of three children's television programs that were popular during the 1980s. The first was *The Kids of Degrassi Street*, which was on television from 1979 to 1986. The series was filmed in Toronto and used Canadian child actors. *Degrassi Junior High* and *Degrassi High* followed. These later series featured many of the same actors. The Degrassi programs were very popular with children and adults alike. The series often dealt with serious issues, including peer pressure and divorce.

Second City

Second City Television made its debut in 1976. It was a show that made fun of television and its celebrities. It was set in a fictional television station called SCTV, and presented skits of **mock** newscasts, talk shows, and television specials. The series was drawn from The Second City, a live comedy troupe that performed in Toronto. As the show went on, it grew in popularity. By the end of its run in 1983, it had been nominated for thirteen Emmy Awards, and had won two. There were 185 half-hour episodes produced.

▬▬ John Candy became a recognized face on *SCTV* before making it big in American movies.

SCTV was written and performed mainly by Canadian talent. Many *SCTV* cast members got their acting start on the Canadian program, and they went on to become famous movie actors. John Candy,

Martin Short, Eugene Levy, Dave Thomas, Rick Moranis, and Catherine O'Hara are a few of the *SCTV* originals who made a name for themselves in film. Also, several *SCTV* characters, such as Martin Short's character Ed Grimley, followed the actors to other comedy programs, including *Saturday Night Live.*

Take Off, Eh!

One *SCTV* skit became especially popular. Dave Thomas and Rick Moranis played two "hoser" Canadian brothers, Bob and Doug McKenzie. They exaggerated some Canadian features. They wore plaid shirts and toques, and spoke with strong Canadian accents. Bob and Doug became so popular that a movie called *Strange Brew* was created to feature these characters.

Expo 86

Expo is an international fair that is held in a different country every few years. From May to October 1986, Expo 86 was held in Vancouver, British Columbia. At that time, it was the largest exposition ever held.

The themes of Expo 86 were transportation and communication. Its slogan was "World in Motion—World in Touch."

▬▬ The Science Centre was one of the most popular attractions at Expo 86.

The area for the fair included a covered stadium, a theatre, and the Plaza of Nations. There were sixty-four different pavilions, or displays. The Northwest Territories was one of the most popular pavilions. It was built of light blue plaster and glass and looked like it contained real icebergs and

glaciers. It had displays and films to show visitors what life was like for people in the Canadian North.

Expo 86 had 8,000 volunteers to help out throughout the fair. A monorail was built to move people around the exposition site. The monorail moved 10.5 million passengers throughout the fair.

Although the exposition lost money, many businesses made money from the many new visitors to the area. Expo 86 was considered to be a great success for Canada, and it launched Vancouver into a new era of growth and expansion.

Anne of Green Gables

In 1985, a television mini-series was created based on Lucy Maud Montgomery's well-known Canadian children's book, *Anne of Green Gables*. Many Canadian children and adults had read the book. The television show introduced the feisty redheaded orphan named Anne to thousands of others. The director of the movie auditioned 3,000 girls in search of the right actress to play Anne. He finally hired Megan Follows, a sixteen-year-old actress from Toronto. The mini-series was a huge hit. It was eventually seen by millions of people in 145 different countries. It won awards

▥ *Anne of Green Gables* **is very popular in Japan. It earned more money than most American movies while playing in Japanese theatres.**

in Canada and the United States. *Anne of Green Gables* became one of the most successful Canadian mini-series of all time.

A Canadian Filmmaker

Many of Hollywood's most popular films owe a great deal to Canadians in one way or another. During the 1980s, Norman Jewison directed several movies. Norman was born in Toronto. He began his career as an actor at the age of five. Norman later became a director and producer of films.

In 1984, Norman directed a film called *A Soldier's Story*. The next year, he directed *Agnes of God*. Each film was nominated for three Academy Awards. The 1987 film *Moonstruck* was perhaps Norman's most popular film. Starring Cher and Nicholas Cage, *Moonstruck* won three Academy Awards and was a box-office success.

Norman also began to work with young people interested in film. In 1986, he opened the Canadian Centre for Advanced Film Studies in Toronto. This school helps young directors, producers, and screenwriters get a start in film. Norman was made a Companion to the Order of Canada in 1982.

The Magic of Michael J. Fox

A young actor from Canada made a big splash in Hollywood during the 1980s. Michael J. Fox began acting on Canadian television as a teenager. A casting director convinced him to move to Los Angeles. His youthful appearance meant that he could play characters who were much younger than himself. When Michael was cast as Alex P. Keaton in *Family Ties*, he became one of America's favourite sons. Michael quickly became the show's most popular personality. He won Emmy Awards in 1986, 1987, and 1988 for his work.

Michael also showed that he could be successful in movies. He starred in the 1985 film *Back to the Future* as a teenager who travels back in time. The movie was so popular that two sequels followed in 1989 and 1990.

"I brought my first Emmy home to give to my parents and I put it on the table by the front door. When I woke up the next morning, my brother's boxing trophy, my sister's bowling trophy, and my mom's bridge trophy were on a table next to it."

Michael J. Fox

"Look Up … Waayy Up"

Millions of Canadian children grew up watching and listening to Bob Homme, who played the Friendly Giant in the television show of the same name. *The Friendly Giant* ran from 1958 until it went off the air in 1984. Bob played the part of a giant who lived in a castle.

▥ *The Friendly Giant* was a fifteen-minute show that first aired in the United States before moving to the Canadian Broadcasting Corporation (CBC).

Friendly was surrounded by his pals Rusty the Rooster and Jerome the Giraffe, both puppets. On every episode, Friendly played an instrument, such as a recorder or a clarinet, while Rusty "played" the harp and Jerome sang along.

The Beachcombers

Starting in 1972, *The Beachcombers* became one of Canada's longest-running television shows. The series was about a middle-aged beachcomber who lived on the coast of British Columbia. Canadians spent the entire decade absorbed in the activities of Nick, Jesse, Relic, and the gang of Molly's Reach. *The Beachcombers* was also popular in other countries, such as the United Kingdom and Australia. The series was cancelled in 1991.

▥ Actor Bruno Gerussi, who played Nick Adonidas on *The Beachcombers*, helped make it one of the most successful series in Canada.

"Who're You Gonna Call?"

The film *Ghostbusters* was one of the most popular comedies of the 1980s. Although *Ghostbusters* was a big Hollywood film, it was created by Canadian Dan Ackroyd. As a child, Dan thought he had seen ghosts in a farmhouse. For many years, he wanted to write a film script about ghosts. In the beginning, the film was called "Ghostmashers." Dan could not find anyone who wanted to make the film. After rewriting the

▥ Bill Murray, Dan Ackroyd, and Harold Ramis were the men to call in *Ghostbusters*.

script many times, Columbia pictures in Hollywood decided to make the film.

The comedy follows a group of men who help people get rid of ghosts in their homes. The men are then called upon to save the city of New York from being taken over by the deadly spirits. Canadian Rick Moranis also starred in the film alongside Ackroyd. *Ghostbusters* made more than $225 million.

Mega Malls

▰ Visitors to West Edmonton Mall can enjoy a dolphin show or take a submarine ride.

During the eighties, larger and more shopping centres were built across the country. Canadians liked being able to do their shopping indoors in one large building. In 1981, West Edmonton Mall opened. The mall was the largest in the world. It was built in three stages. When it was completed, it contained over 800 stores, many restaurants, a hotel, an amusement park, a lake, a zoo, a water park, a skating rink, and a miniature golf course.

The mall cost $1.1 billion to build, and it is the size of 104 football fields. It contains the world's largest indoor wave pool and an exact copy of the *Santa Maria*, one of Christopher Columbus' ships.

THE RUBIK'S CUBE
Erno Rubik, a professor from Hungary, invented his cube in 1975. He originally created the cube to teach his students about three-dimensional objects. The cube was like a puzzle with movable parts that could twist but not come apart. The goal was to match all the small, coloured squares on the sides of the cube. Professor Rubik sold his cube around the world. The cube was especially popular in the United States and Canada. In 1980, more than 4.5 million cubes were sold. Even more sold the next year.

Many people found it very difficult, if not impossible, to solve the Rubik's Cube. Over sixty books were published that gave hints on how to solve the puzzle. Other people formed clubs, and competitions were held all over the world. During one competition in Budapest, Hungary, a contestant solved the puzzle in just 55 seconds. There were reports of it being solved in even less time.

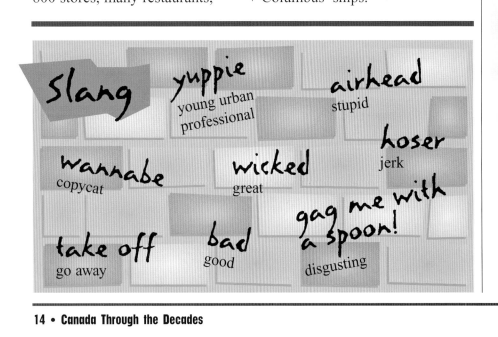

Slang

yuppie
young urban professional

airhead
stupid

wannabe
copycat

wicked
great

hoser
jerk

take off
go away

bad
good

gag me with a spoon!
disgusting

Computer Arcades

Very few people had computers or computer games in the early part of the decade. Instead, young people would go to arcades to play computer games. Pac-Man and similar games took up the time and money of many children and teens. Arcades were a place where young people could go and meet friends.

In the later part of the decade, more people began to play computer games in their own homes. Atari and Colecovision were the two most popular home entertainment systems. With Atari, children played games

▥ Atari 400 allowed people to play popular games such as Pac-Man and Frogger, or to program their own game using the keyboard.

such as Asteroids and Space Invaders for hours on end. Colecovision offered slightly better graphics with games such as Donkey Kong and Ladybug.

Breakdancing

Breakdancing is a style of dancing unlike any other. Some of it is done on the floor with the dancer spinning in circles on his or her head or back. Breakdancing was a big hit during the 1980s. It first became popular with young African American males in New York City. Different breakdancers would often compete to see who could invent the best dance. Michael Jackson helped to introduce breakdancing to the rest of the world. He would often use breakdancing moves in his concerts and music videos.

The Cabbage Patch Doll

In 1983, one doll above all others caused riots in stores. Parents were desperate to buy a Cabbage Patch doll for their children for Christmas. Each Cabbage Patch doll was slightly different from the others. Every doll came with a name and adoption certificate. The owner of the doll became the adoptive "parent."

▥ People were so eager to buy Cabbage Patch dolls that some stores wrapped the dolls in paper to prevent people from fighting over particular features.

Chernobyl

In 1986, a nuclear power station in Chernobyl, Ukraine, began to leak radioactive waste. Radioactive waste is very dangerous to humans. The Soviet government waited a few days before telling anyone. Chernobyl became the world's worst nuclear disaster. Many people who lived near the power plant became ill from **radiation** sickness. Others suffered from radiation burns.

Clouds of radioactive material floated to other countries, such as Sweden and Poland. In Poland, farm workers became sick and lost their hair. Many birds died after coming into contact with the radioactive clouds. People all over Europe were told not to consume fresh water, fruits, vegetables, or even milk. By 1988, thirty-one people had died because of the accident. Hundreds of others became ill.

Many of the Ukrainian people who lived close to the accident site were forced to leave their homes. Areas near the power plant will be unsafe for people for decades.

▥ After the Chernobyl disaster, nearby residents had to be tested for abnormal radioactive levels.

Tiananmen Square

In June of 1989, 1 million student protesters in China gathered in Tiananmen Square in the city of Beijing. The protesters did not like the way the government was run. They wanted China to become more **democratic**. Students built a statue in the square and called it the "Goddess of Democracy." The Chinese government warned the students to leave the area. When this did not happen, military units were sent in to control the protesters. Thousands of people were killed or arrested. People around the world were shocked by the treatment of the peaceful protesters.

▥ The Chinese government has never officially said how many people died during the Tiananmen Square massacre, but many observers guessed the death toll was around 3,000.

A ROYAL WEDDING

▥ On July 29, 1981, 700 million people around the world watched the wedding of Charles, Prince of Wales and Lady Diana Spencer. It was called a fairy-tale wedding because of its size and grandeur. There were three orchestras playing and a choir singing. Thousands of Canadians got up in the middle of the night to watch the wedding live on television. Many Canadians came to think of Diana as Canada's princess, because her birthday, July 1, was the same day as Canada Day.

The Fall of the Berlin Wall

In 1961, the city of Berlin was divided by two countries, East Germany and West Germany. East Germany had been a communist country with strict rules for its citizens. Many East Germans were escaping to West Germany in Berlin. The East German government built a wall through the city to prevent these escapes. The wall separated Germans who lived in East and West Berlin. Some people could no longer have any contact with family members who lived on the other side of the wall. People who tried to escape to West Berlin were often shot by border guards. More than 170 people died trying to escape.

During the early 1980s, relations between East and West Germany improved. The East

▥ **Thousands of people chipped away pieces of the Berlin Wall to keep as souvenirs.**

German government began to allow their people more freedom. In 1989, as the **Cold War** came to an end, the East German government decided to open up the wall. The East German people were allowed to come and go as they pleased. People from East and West Germany rushed

to the wall to celebrate. Some climbed over it while others danced on top of it. Many people chipped away pieces of the wall. Relatives and friends who had not seen one another in years were finally able to meet.

For people around the world, the wall coming down was a sign of peace. The following year, East and West Germany united to become one country.

Libya and the United States

Libya is a country in the Middle East. During the 1980s, relations between Libya and the United States were very tense. At times, it seemed as if there might be a war between the two countries. The American president, Ronald Reagan, believed that Libya was supporting terrorists. Muammar al-Qadhafi, the leader of Libya, felt that the U.S. was trying to overthrow his government.

In 1986, the U.S. broke off all economic ties with Libya. That same year, Libya fired missiles at U.S. aircraft that were flying over

▥ **Muammar al-Qadhafi was America's "public enemy number one" during the 1980s.**

nearby water. The U.S. believed that Libya made several terrorist attacks on Americans around the world. They discovered that Libya was likely responsible for the bombing of a nightclub in

West Germany. An American was killed and many others injured in this terrorist act. President Reagan decided to bomb military areas in Libya. Other countries did not agree that this was the correct action to take.

The problems between Libya and the U.S. continued until the end of the decade. In 1989, American planes shot down two Libyan jets. The United States defended their action. The pilots of the American planes claimed that the Libyan jets were about to attack them.

Man of the Decade

Soviet President Mikhail Gorbachev was chosen as "Man of the Decade" by *Time* magazine. Gorbachev was elected leader of the Communist party of the Soviet Union in 1985. President Gorbachev started to make changes to the country immediately. He abandoned many of the beliefs on which the communist Soviet Union had been founded. He removed Soviet troops from Afghanistan. He also encouraged many Soviet republics to become independent. He improved relations with other countries in the world, particularly the United States. He was the major reason for the end of the Cold War among the Soviet Union and countries in the West. President Gorbachev also led the way for Russia to become a democracy.

▦ **Mikhail Gorbachev held many meetings with Western leaders to discuss democracy. He also met with Pope John Paul II.**

Glasnost

Glasnost means "openness" in Russian. In the 1980s, the Soviet Union became more open with the rest of the world than it had been in decades. President Mikhail Gorbachev was responsible for *glasnost* in the USSR. Under *glasnost*, the Soviet media was free for the first time in decades to discuss the country's problems openly.

Areas in the Soviet Union that were not inhabited by Russians, such as the Ukraine, were allowed to become independent of the USSR. These changes continued throughout the decade. Eventually they led to the collapse of the Soviet Union as a world superpower.

Russia

Ukraine

▦ **The Ukraine was able to become an independent country after Gorbachev introduced *glasnost*.**

Oil Spill

The *Exxon Valdez* was an oil tanker for a large American oil company. The tanker was used to transport oil from an Alaskan pipeline to the rest of the United States. In 1989, the *Exxon Valdez* collided with a reef in the water. The impact of the collision tore apart the tanker. Oil poured out of the *Exxon Valdez* and into the Arctic waters. In total, 42 million litres of oil spilled from the tanker. It was one of the worst oil spills in history.

The oil had a devastating effect on the environment. Thousands of birds and sea otters died. Some of the birds drowned. Covered in the heavy oil, the birds could not float or fly. Other birds and otters froze to death.

▥ Once repaired, the former *Exxon Valdez* became the *Exxon Mediterranean*.

"I'd say the lesson to society is that a spill like this can happen. No matter how low the probability, the potential is still there."

Frank Iarossi, former shipping president, Exxon

Most animals died because they ate plants covered in the toxic oil. Rescuers and volunteers rushed to the area to try to save birds and animals that were still alive. They captured the animals and cleaned the oil off their bodies.

The spilled oil also affected fish. The fish in the area could not be collected for food because they would be too dangerous to eat. This had a terrible effect on the many people who fished for a living.

Exxon tried to clean up after the spill, but winds blew the oil over a 250-square-kilometre area. It was impossible to repair all the damage done by the spill.

Canadian Caper

In 1977, Ken Taylor was appointed the Canadian ambassador to Iran. Three years later he became an international hero. In 1980, revolutionaries in Iran took over the United States embassy. They held sixty-six people hostage. Six American **diplomats** escaped from the hostage holders, but their lives were still in danger. Taylor and another Canadian Embassy official hid the six people in their homes in Iran.

Over the next few months, Taylor kept the diplomats safe. With Taylor's help, the diplomats escaped the country by pretending to be Canadian movie producers. As soon as they were safe, Taylor closed down the Canadian Embassy and left Iran as well. Taylor was called a hero, particularly by people in the United States. For his bravery, he was awarded both the Order of Canada and the U.S. Congressional Gold Medal.

▥ Ken Taylor was named the Canadian consul general in New York from 1981 to 1984.

Famine in Africa

In 1984 and 1985, the African nation of Ethiopia experienced a terrible **drought**. Crops in the area died off, leaving no food for many Ethiopian people. Millions of people were in danger of starving to death. News of the tragedy spread to wealthier countries. Images of dying children were shown on television. Nations around the world rushed to deliver food to the area. About 5.8 million Ethiopians needed this relief food.

The Quebec Referendum

In 1976, the Parti Québécois (PQ) was elected in Quebec. The PQ believed that Quebec should not be a part of Canada. In 1980, this government held a **referendum**. They asked Quebeckers to decide whether or not they wanted to be part of Canada. The PQ felt Quebec should embrace **sovereignty-**association. This meant the province would be a

separate nation with close ties to Canada. Sixty percent of Quebec residents voted to remain in Canada. The PQ continued to promote separation, but English Quebeckers and groups outside the province became less sympathetic. The economy faltered, and Quebeckers voted the Liberal party back into office in 1985.

▬ Claude Ryan of the Quebec Liberal party made a victory speech after the referendum vote.

Quebec Language Laws

In 1977, the Quebec government passed a law stating that only the French language could be used by government and businesses in Quebec. This law, Bill 101, was made to help protect the French language and culture in Quebec. Bill 101 made many English-speaking Quebeckers angry. New immigrants to Canada also found the law frustrating. If they wanted to live in Quebec, Bill 101 demanded that their children go to French-language schools and learn to speak French. In 1980, the Supreme Court of Canada decided that Quebec could not make French the only official language in courts and government.

In 1988, the Quebec government took their language laws even further. It became illegal to post signs in any language other than French. One man complained to the United

Nations about the law. The U.N. Human Rights Committee decided the law violated freedom of expression. Eventually the law was changed. People could have other languages on their signs, but the French words had to be more noticeable.

▬ Gordon McIntyre was forced to remove his English-language sign in Huntingdon, Quebec.

O CANADA!

▬ The song "O Canada" is an important Canadian symbol. It was first sung in 1880. The music was written by Calixa Lavallee, who was once known as Canada's national musician. By 1914, "O Canada" was the best-known patriotic song about the country. For decades, "God Save the Queen" was the official national anthem. Despite this, "O Canada" was sung in schools, at sports events, and at special government occasions. Finally, on July 1, 1980, "O Canada" was officially proclaimed Canada's national anthem.

The Canadian Constitution

In 1982, Queen Elizabeth II proclaimed the Constitution Act of Canada. This Act meant that, for the first time since its 1867 confederation, Canada had its own constitution. Canada became completely independent from Great Britain. It could make changes to its laws without permission from the queen.

Prime Minister Pierre Trudeau hoped to create a constitution that would work for all Canadians. The Constitution Act contains the Canadian Charter of Rights and Freedoms. This charter lists thirty-four rights of all Canadians, including freedom of speech and religion. All provinces except Quebec agreed to accept the constitution.

■ Queen Elizabeth II signed the Constitution Act despite Quebec's belief that the Act left the province in a much weaker state.

Meech Lake Accord

René Lévesque, the premier of Quebec, did not sign the 1982 constitution. Premier Levesque and his political party, the Parti Québécois, wanted Quebec to separate from Canada. The PQ wanted nothing to do with Prime Minister Trudeau's Canadian constitution.

The Canadian government wanted Quebec to agree to the constitution. In 1986, Quebec elected Robert Bourassa and the Liberal party to government. Premier Bourassa was interested in trying to come to an agreement with the rest of Canada. In 1987, led by Prime Minister Mulroney, the provincial premiers created the Meech Lake Accord. This agreement stated that Canada was a bilingual country. It also recognized Quebec as a distinct society. If the Accord was passed, Quebec agreed to be part of the constitution.

All provinces had to agree to the Accord within three years. Quebec was happy with the agreement. Two other provinces, however, did not pass the Accord. Newfoundland wanted more time to get the opinions of its citizens. In Manitoba, Aboriginal leaders wanted the Accord to be changed to recognize the importance of Aboriginal Peoples in Canada. By 1990, the Meech Lake Accord had collapsed.

■ The Meech Lake Accord appeared to be a success when it was first created in 1987. However, changes in provincial governments also changed premiers' attitudes toward the Accord.

The Mulroney Era

▥▥▥ Brian Mulroney, here with his wife Mila, was the first Conservative prime minister since John A. MacDonald to win two successive majority victories.

In 1984, after nearly fifteen years of Liberal leadership in the prime minister's office, Brian Mulroney and the Progressive Conservative (PC) party were voted into power. They won 211 of the 282 seats in parliament. Mulroney made his mark in Canada with his hard-hitting policies and initiatives. Among these were the Goods and Services Tax (GST) and deficit fighting, both of which Prime Minister Jean Chretien continued to implement when he came into office.

Mulroney also helped bring about the **controversial** Free Trade Agreement with the United States, and the North American Free Trade Agreement with Mexico. He attempted to address Quebec's concerns with his distinct society policy. Although both the Meech Lake and Charlottetown Accords failed, they proved that Canada had to find a constitutional solution for Quebec. Mulroney's government alienated many Canadians. The rise of the Reform party in Western Canada and the Bloc Québécois in Quebec were both partly due to Canadians' dissatisfaction with Mulroney ignoring regional concerns. Brian Mulroney was voted into office for two straight terms, but he was, at the end of his nine years, the most unpopular national leader in Canadian polling history.

Elections

In 1980, Pierre Trudeau and the Liberal party were elected to lead the country. Canadians were becoming disillusioned with the government, and the PC party also won many seats. At the 1984 election, Brian Mulroney and his PC party won a majority government. The party won again, with less of a lead, in 1988.

Federal Election Results
(number of seats in Parliament)

	1980	1984	1988
Liberal Party	147	40	83
Progressive Conservative Party	103	211	169
New Democrat Party	32	30	43
Other Parties	0	1	0
Total number of seats	282	282	295

WOMEN IN POLITICS

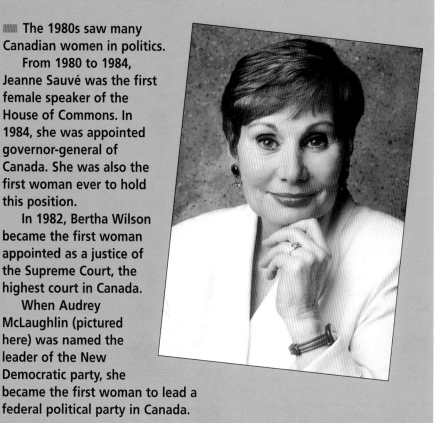

▓ The 1980s saw many Canadian women in politics.

From 1980 to 1984, Jeanne Sauvé was the first female speaker of the House of Commons. In 1984, she was appointed governor-general of Canada. She was also the first woman ever to hold this position.

In 1982, Bertha Wilson became the first woman appointed as a justice of the Supreme Court, the highest court in Canada.

When Audrey McLaughlin (pictured here) was named the leader of the New Democratic party, she became the first woman to lead a federal political party in Canada.

Alberta's Seat Belt Law

In 1989, Alberta passed a law requiring everyone to wear a seat belt whenever they were in a vehicle. Many citizens complained about the law. Some claimed the law infringed on their civil rights. These people argued that each person should decide whether he or she would wear a seat belt. Some people even claimed that seatbelts could pose a danger in automobile accidents.

One man, Kim Maier, decided to challenge the new law. He took the province to court to try to defeat the seat belt law. Kim argued that the government had no right to force him to wear a seat belt if he did not want to. Eventually, Kim lost his fight.

Righting a Wrong

During World War II, after the Japanese bombed Pearl Harbor, life for Japanese Canadians was difficult. All Japanese Canadians, even those who had been born in Canada, were removed from their homes. Their belongings were taken from them, and they were placed in detention camps. They were treated badly simply because of their ethnic background. Many Canadians are ashamed by this historical treatment of Japanese Canadians. During the 1980s, the Canadian government took action to repay those people whose lives were turned upside down during the war.

For several years, the government tried to reach an agreement with the National Association of Japanese Canadians. In September of 1988, Prime Minister Mulroney announced that Canada would pay $21,000 to each Canadian who had been interned during the war. The Canadian government

▓ Japanese Canadians interned during the war lived in poor, crowded conditions.

also formally apologized for its actions against Japanese Canadians during World War II.

Storyteller Extraordinaire

Children's publishing grew in Canada during the 1980s. One notable reason for this was children's author and storyteller Robert Munsch. Munsch was born in the United States, but he became a Canadian after he and his wife moved to Canada during the seventies.

Munsch always loved to tell stories. He decided to try and write his stories down on paper. In 1979, a Canadian publisher, Annick Press, agreed to publish Munch's first book, *Mud Puddle*. The next year, *The Paper Bag Princess* was published. This popular story about a girl who outsmarts a dragon to save her prince was an instant hit. Munsch wrote many other children's books, including *Murmel, Murmel, Murmel* and *Thomas' Snowsuit*. His books have sold millions of copies around the world.

> "I wrote down ten stories and sent them off to ten different publishers. Nine said, 'No' and one said, 'Yes' to a story called *Mud Puddle*."
>
> Robert Munsch

1913–1995

Robertson Davies

Robertson Davies was one of the best-known Canadian writers for decades. Davies began his career as an actor. He was also a teacher. Davies wrote many novels, plays, and **nonfiction** books. In 1985, three of his most popular books were published in one volume called *The Deptford Trilogy*. In 1986, his book *What's Bred in the Bone* won the Canadian Authors Association Literary Award for fiction. The book was also nominated for Britain's prestigious Booker Prize. *What's Bred in the Bone* was the second book of three called the Cornish series.

> "A truly great book should be read in youth, again in maturity, and once more in old age...."
>
> Robertson Davies

A Turtle Named Franklin

Many Canadian children's books written during the 1980s became popular around the world. In 1986, *Franklin in the Dark* was published. This picture book featured a young turtle who was so afraid of the dark that he hated being in his shell. The book was written by Paulette Bourgeois and illustrated by Brenda Clark. Bourgeois decided to write a children's book when her daughter, Natalie, was one month old. Franklin was such a popular character that Bourgeois and Clark created many other books about him. *Hurry Up, Franklin* was published in 1989.

By 1999, Bourgeois and Clark had created over fifteen Franklin books.

W.P. Kinsella

Although W.P. (Bill) Kinsella did not publish his first stories until he was forty-two years old, he is one of Canada's greatest authors. Kinsella wrote short stories, novels, and articles. He first became known for a group of short stories he wrote about a character named Silas, a Cree man. In 1982, he published his most popular novel, *Shoeless Joe.* It is about a man, Ray, who is driven to mow down his cornfield to make a baseball field, where the spirits of the 1919 Chicago White Sox baseball team come to play. Although Kinsella is Canadian, many people in the United States think *Shoeless Joe* is the best novel written about America's favourite pastime. In 1989, *Shoeless Joe* was made into a major Hollywood film, *Field of Dreams*, starring Kevin Costner.

Kinsella wrote several collections of short stories during the 1980s. He also wrote another popular novel about baseball, *The Iowa Baseball Confederacy*.

▩ Bill Kinsella gave his lead character in *Shoeless Joe* the name Ray Kinsella.

BOOK AND MOVIE

▩ Poet and novelist Margaret Atwood wrote many popular novels over the decades. One of her best-known books, *The Handmaid's Tale,* was written in 1985. It won several awards and was made into a Hollywood film. The novel is a work of science fiction that contains a world in which women have few rights.

Writing about Canada

"History books should read as much like novels as possible."

Pierre Berton

Pierre Berton writes nonfiction books about Canada. His history books are not dry and dull, but are always full of interesting stories. During the 1980s, Berton wrote *The Klondike Quest*, which was about the search for gold in the Canadian North. *The Promised Land* explained the settlement of the West in the early part of the century. *Vimy* told about Canadians during World War I. *The Arctic Grail* was a popular book about the exploration of Canada. In 1989, Berton published *Starting Out, 1920–1947*, which was the first volume of his **autobiography**.

First Canadian in Space

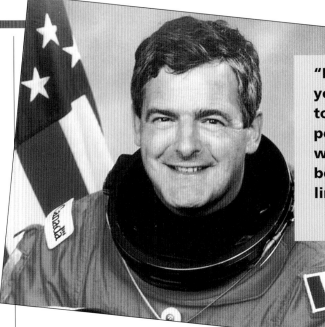

Marc Garneau became one of only six Canadians selected to train as astronauts in 1983. He became the first Canadian to travel into space on a mission the following year. Garneau flew on one of **NASA's** space shuttle missions. On this trip, Garneau and six other astronauts spent eight days aboard the space shuttle *Challenger*. They circled Earth 133 times. Marc did several scientific experiments while on the shuttle.

> "Believe in yourself and dare to stretch ten percent beyond what you believe is your limit."
>
> Marc Garneau

▇ Before Marc Garneau became an astronaut, he was a naval officer in the Canadian Armed Forces.

Learning About Cystic Fibrosis

Cystic fibrosis (CF) is a disease passed on from parents to children. People suffering from CF rarely live longer than twenty-five years. On May 9, 1989, Dr. Lap-Chee Tsui, a scientist from Toronto, helped discover the **gene** that causes cystic fibrosis. It took five more months to make sure that the discovery was correct. By September, Dr. Tsui and his team of scientists knew that they had found the CF gene.

Dr. Tsui's work helped other scientists understand how CF works. The discovery meant that doctors could then predict whether or not a couple is likely to have a child with CF. One day, there may be new treatments or even a cure for cystic fibrosis.

> "Knowing science can enrich your life."
>
> Dr. Lap-Chee Tsui

CANADARM

▇ Canadarm is a piece of equipment that is used by astronauts. It allows astronauts to retrieve and use other equipment, such as **satellites**, in space. Canadarm was designed and built in Canada. It has helped Canada become a world leader in space robotics.

The first Canadarm was built in 1981. It cost nearly $100 million to create. It was first tested on a NASA space shuttle flight in November. The Canadarm worked perfectly. Since then, Canadarm has been used during many space shuttle flights. It allows astronauts to perform many tasks they could not otherwise do.

HALLEY'S COMET

During 1985 and the first few months of 1986, people around the world waited to hear news about Halley's comet. Perhaps the most famous comet, Halley's was named after Edmund Halley, the scientist who discovered that the comet had a seventy-six-year orbit. This means that the comet can be seen only once every seventy-six years.

In 1984 and 1985, five spacecraft were sent up to meet the approaching comet. Scientists discovered that Halley's comet was about 16 kilometres long, 8 kilometres high, and 8 kilometres wide. People hoped that they would be able to see the comet in the sky. Unfortunately, the comet was not visible to skywatchers in Canada. People who lived in the Southern Hemisphere did not get a good look at the comet either because it travelled too close to the Sun.

▦ Home computers, such as this Apple IIe, were often used for word processing and simple programs.

Personal Computers

Computers had been around for many years. They were much too big and difficult for the average person to use. In the 1980s, the "personal computer" (PC) was created. The PC was small and inexpensive. People bought the computers to use at work and in their homes.

Computers became popular very quickly. In 1981, Canadians spent $150 million on PCs compared to $1.18 billion spent in 1985. Many schools bought computers for students to use.

"By the end of 1982, there were 2,200 computer stores in the United States, and sales of personal computers in this market reached 810,000 units. Worldwide, the personal computer market grew 71 percent to $4.3 billion."

Portia Isacson, computer industry employee

Computers soon began to replace typewriters. They were also used to communicate with other computers. Universities and businesses began to use computers to get information from other institutions. The Internet was also available, although it would not become popular for home use until the 1990s. In 1984, a Canadian author, William Gibson, created the word **cyberspace** to describe the Internet.

DNA Fingerprinting

In 1985, scientists learned how to match a **DNA** sample to a person. This discovery helped law officials solve many crimes that could have otherwise gone unsolved. A strand of hair or spot of blood left at a crime scene could now prove that a person was there. For a Canadian man, it proved that he was not there.

David Milgaard spent twenty-two years in prison for a murder he insisted he did not commit. Using the advancements in DNA research, Milgaard was finally proven innocent and released from prison.

The Great One

Wayne Gretzky learned how to skate at the age of two on a rink his father made in the backyard. By the time he was six, he was playing hockey with boys five and six years older. During the 1980s, Gretzky was the most exciting player in the National Hockey League. With the Edmonton Oilers, Gretzky won the Stanley Cup four years in a row. He won the Hart Memorial Trophy, given to the most valuable player for the season, for eight years during the decade. In 1989, Gretzky broke Gordie Howe's 1,850-point record of most points scored.

▥ In the 1982–83 season, Wayne Gretzky scored ninety-two goals.

Terry Fox and the Marathon of Hope

On April 12, 1980, Terry Fox dipped his artificial leg into the Atlantic Ocean. It was the beginning of his Marathon of Hope, a run across Canada to raise awareness and funds for cancer. Fox had lost his leg to bone cancer.

For 143 days, Fox ran an average of 26 miles a day. He made it two-thirds of the way across Canada before his run was cut short. Fox's cancer had returned—this time to his lungs. Although Fox hoped to beat cancer again and finish his run, he died on June 28, 1981 at the age of twenty-two.

Fox had raised $24.2 million for cancer research. More importantly, he inspired many cancer survivors around the world with his spirit. Every year, Terry Fox runs are held across Canada to help raise more money for cancer research.

▥ Rick Hansen's Man in Motion World Tour raised $20 million for spinal cord research, rehabilitation, and wheelchair sports.

Man in Motion

Rick Hansen was a world-class wheelchair athlete. Inspired by his friend, Terry Fox, he wanted to raise money to help people with disabilities. He decided to travel around the world in his wheelchair. Hansen left Vancouver in 1985 on his Man in Motion tour. He travelled through thirty-four countries, ending his tour back in Canada. His entire trip lasted 792 days. He wore out 117 tires on his wheelchair and eleven pairs of gloves. His Man in Motion tour raised money for research and **rehabilitation** of people with disabilities.

Calgary Winter Olympics

In February 1988, the Winter Olympics were held in and around Calgary, Alberta. The games brought athletes from around the world. In total, 1,423 athletes from fifty-seven countries participated in the games. The athletes competed in a variety of sports, including ski jumping and ice skating. Calgary and Alberta spent a great deal of money getting ready for the games. A new skating oval was built, as well as Canada Olympic Park, an area with ski jumps and bobsled runs.

Thousands of volunteers helped out during the games. The international athletes enjoyed the Canadian landscape and hospitality. The games were a great success.

▦ Robyn Perry was selected over eight other children to carry the torch for the final leg of its journey.

The Olympic Torch Relay

Many Canadians applied for the chance to carry the Olympic Torch as it travelled across Canada to the Calgary Olympic Games. Over 6.5 million forms were sent to the Olympic committee. In the end, 6,520 people were chosen to be torch-bearers. Each torch-bearer travelled 1 kilometre. The torch began its journey in Newfoundland in November of 1987. It completed its journey when it reached Calgary to officially open the Olympics.

Robyn Perry was the lucky person who was the final torch-bearer. Perry was a twelve-year-old student in Calgary. She was chosen to symbolize youth and future Olympians. As 2 billion people watched on television, Perry carried the Olympic torch up a steep staircase. At the top of the stairs, she reached up and lit the 1988 Olympic cauldron that burned throughout the games. Perry became a Canadian celebrity. For the rest of the year, she made over 100 public appearances talking about her experience with the torch.

▦ Sixty thousand people packed McMahon Stadium to celebrate the Opening Ceremonies, while 2 billion people watched the event on television.

DRUGS AND SPORTS

▦ Canadians watched with anticipation as runner Ben Johnson became the fastest man in the world. Johnson won a gold medal for the 100-metre race at the 1988 Olympics in Seoul, South Korea. He broke his own world record with a time of 9.79 seconds. It was soon discovered that Johnson had been taking **steroids** to improve his running. Steroids are a banned substance for athletes. Johnson's gold medal and world record were taken away from him. He was banned from competing for two years. His coach, Charlie Francis, had encouraged Johnson and other athletes to take steroids. Francis was banned from coaching for life. This story made people aware that athletes sometimes took illegal drugs to improve their performance.

▌ Big Ben is an honorary member of the RCMP Musical Ride.

The Amazing Oilers

With Wayne Gretzky as their leader, the Edmonton Oilers were the most exciting team to watch during the 1980s. Gretzky signed on with the young Oilers team when he was eighteen years old. Edmonton was considered a hockey city. The fans were thrilled to get an NHL team.

As well as Gretzky, the Oilers team was full of other talented players. Mark Messier, Glenn Anderson, Jari Kurri, and Paul Coffey were some of the league's best players. The young players were full of energy and enthusiasm. They were all good friends who worked well as a team under coach Glen Sather. The team focussed on offensive plays in a league that felt the best teams had strong defensive abilities.

The Oilers won the Stanley Cup in 1984, 1985, 1987, and 1988. Hockey fans argue over which team was the best in NHL history. Few disagree that the Oilers of the 1980s were the most exciting.

The Legendary Big Ben

Big Ben is not only a famous bell in London, England. It is also the name of a special horse—the horse was named Big Ben because of its enormous size. In 1983, Canadian show jumper Ian Millar bought Big Ben and brought him to Canada. In 1984, Big Ben came in second place in his first grand prix equestrian competition. Ian and Big Ben were members of the fourth-place team at the Los Angeles Olympics later that year.

During the next decade, Ian and Big Ben won dozens of other competitions. Together, they became the first to win the World Cup title twice in a row, in 1988 and 1989. Big Ben had become a Canadian celebrity. Fans would send him letters and bran muffins—his favourite food. Big Ben retired from professional jumping in 1994.

City of Champions

Edmonton, Alberta, erected a sign in the 1980s stating it was the "City of Champions" to welcome visitors to the city. In that decade, Edmonton was home to two championship professional sports teams.

The Oilers won four Stanley Cups during the decade. In the Canadian Football League, the Edmonton Eskimos also won top honours—the Grey Cup—four times, in 1980, 1981, 1982, and 1987.

▌ Edmonton's "City of Champions" sign greets visitors who enter the city on Highway 2—the link between Edmonton and Calgary.

The Crazy Canucks

From the mid-seventies to the early eighties, the Canadian National Ski Team was the best in the world. The male members of the team were nicknamed the Crazy Canucks. They included "Jungle" Jim Hunter, Dave Irwin, Dave Murray, Ken Read, and Steve Podborski. The Canadian team dominated downhill skiing like they never had before, or since. A male or female Canadian skier won a World Cup event in every year during the 1980s.

Crazy Canuck members Dave Murray, Ken Read, Steve Podborski, and Dave Irwin with fellow racer Chris Kent in Val d'Isere, France.

The "Flower"

Guy Lafleur was a right winger for the Montreal Canadiens hockey team from 1971 to 1984. He was immensely popular with fans because he was such a joy to watch. Stylish, fast, and with drive to win, the "Flower" was one of the most-loved NHL players of all time.

Lafleur was a top player from the start of his career. During his rookie season in the NHL, he scored sixty-four points in seventy-three games. He was the youngest player to score 400 goals and also the youngest to reach 1,000 points. Lafleur was also the first player to score more than fifty goals a season in six consecutive seasons. During his career, he won the Art Ross trophy three times for being the league points leader, the Conn Smythe trophy twice for being the most valuable player during the playoffs, and the Hart trophy once for the

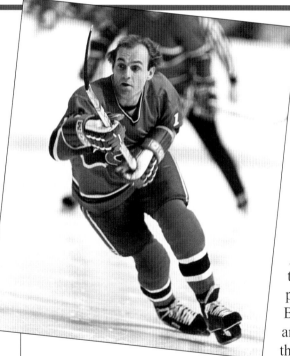

The Montreal Canadiens won the Stanley Cup five times with the help of Guy Lafleur.

most valuable player in the regular season.

In 1988, Lafleur returned to hockey to play a few games with the New York Rangers and the Quebec Nordiques. He officially retired and was inducted into the NHL Hall of Fame that same year.

Toronto Blue Jays

In 1976, Canada got its second professional baseball team. Toronto had wanted a team since Montreal got the Expos in 1968. During their first three years, over 4 million fans attended the Blue Jays games in Toronto. Despite this support, the team played poorly. Finally, in 1980, the Blue Jays turned their game around. Two years later, under the coaching of Bobby Cox, the team had its best year. In 1983, the Blue Jays had their first winning season, with eighty-nine wins to seventy-three losses. They also set a new attendance record at the Toronto stadium of 2 million fans in a single year. In 1985, the Blue Jays won the American League East championship. The team continued to be one of the best teams in the league throughout the decade.

Recession in Canada

Canada did not fall into an economic **depression** in the eighties. Instead, it suffered from a recession. A recession is a period of lowered economic activity. During the 1980s, more Canadians had trouble finding jobs than ever before. The unemployment rate reached 12.9 percent in December 1982. This was higher than it had been since the Depression in the 1930s.

The value of the Canadian dollar dropped compared to the U.S. dollar. In 1986, the Canadian dollar was worth less internationally—70.2 U.S. cents—than it ever had in history. This was just the beginning of a trend that would see the dollar drop much lower during the next decade.

BLACK MONDAY

On October 19, 1987, the New York Stock Exchange had its lowest drop in history. This meant that many people lost a great deal of money in one day. The loss was even worse than the Wall Street crash of 1929 that was the start of the Great Depression. Luckily, the world economy did not suffer from another depression.

Cost of Living

Cost of living means how much money is needed to provide people with homes, food, and other necessities. The cost of living increased greatly from the 1970s to the 1980s. House prices are one way to judge cost of living. From 1975 to 1985, the price of an average home nearly doubled across Canada.

Average Value of Canadian Homes

	1975	1985
Canada	$47,201	$80,775
Toronto	57,583	109,093
Vancouver	57,763	112,852
Mississauga	61,977	99,674
Victoria	n.a.	88,451
Hamilton	45,103	72,972
Ottawa	49,633	107,640
Calgary	48,341	80,462
Montreal	35,266	70,563
Edmonton	43,846	74,309
Halifax	n.a.	79,350
St. John's	n.a.	66,642
Winnipeg	33,463	62,478
Saint John	35,884	57,088
Regina	33,880	61,403

THE LOONIE

In 1987, the Canadian government produced the eleven-sided one-dollar coin. The coin was nicknamed the "loonie" because of the loon on one of its sides.

At first, some Canadians did not like the idea of carrying a heavy coin instead of a dollar bill. Other Canadians were excited by the idea of a new coin. Soon after the coin appeared, the one-dollar bills disappeared and loonies became commonplace.

The National Energy Program

In 1975, most of the Canadian oil industry was owned by people other than Canadians. In 1980, the Canadian government announced a new program to help keep money made from oil and gas in Canada. The National Energy Program (NEP) was made up of three parts. First, the government included its own oil company, PetroCanada, which was created in 1976. It also became more difficult for foreign oil companies to start up in Canada. Second, the government made sure that Canadians could buy oil at prices well under what it was selling for around the world. Third, the government wanted the money made from oil and gas to go to the federal government, not to the provinces.

From the moment the NEP was announced, western Canadians were against it. The oil-rich provinces of the West were forced to sell their oil at lower prices for **domestic** sales. Alberta in particular did not think that the government had a right to interfere in the oil industry. Much of the province's wealth came from oil and gas. The Alberta government accused the federal government of interfering with its powers. Albertans felt robbed by the NEP. When Brian Mulroney was elected in 1984, he met with the premiers of the western provinces. Soon after, the NEP ended.

▥ PetroCanada was a crown corporation and received special advantages in the oil industry.

Devine Government

In 1982, Grant Devine and the Progressive Conservative party were elected to run the Saskatchewan government. Premier Devine stayed in power until 1991. This **Tory** government is now considered one of the most corrupt in Canadian history.

While in power, Premier Devine created a huge **deficit** for Saskatchewan. As it was later discovered, many of the cabinet members were guilty of lying or stealing money from the government. In all, twenty-one members of the Saskatchewan government were charged with crimes committed during the 1980s. Premier Grant Devine was not directly linked to any of the crimes.

However, the government was not all greed and corruption. In an effort to keep the people of Saskatchewan at work during a nation-wide recession, the government developed the Home-owners Grant. It offered money to people to fix up their homes, yards, and neighbourhoods. The government's hope for this project was to foster pride of ownership, neighbourhood development, and the employment of people in a variety of fields. Hospitals were also built across the province for many of the same reasons.

▥ While he was premier of Saskatchewan, Grant Devine tried to attract foreign investment to the province.

Hair Fashions and Head Gear

Just about everyone used a new product—mousse—on their hair in the 1980s. Mousse helped give people the bushy, tousled look that was so popular. Women also crimped their hair with a crimping iron.

Singer Corey Hart made short, spiky hair popular for men. This look also required mousse to get the hair to stand up. This hairstyle was sometimes called a "hedgehog."

Headbands were very popular in the eighties. Both men and women wore them. Mike Reno, the lead singer of the Canadian rock band Loverboy, almost always wore one. John Travolta also wore one in the movie *Staying Alive*. Women usually wore very narrow bands.

▥ Instead of curling irons, women used crimping irons to make kinks in their hair.

▥ John Travolta

If women were not wearing headbands, they might wear a banana clip. Banana clips were used to gather long hair on top of the head.

▥ Corey Hart always wore them. Tom Cruise made them popular in the movie *Risky Business*. People began to wear sunglasses everywhere, even indoors. The most popular brand of sunglasses were Ray Bans.

Madonna Style

American singer Madonna became popular in the mid-eighties. Many of the styles of the decade were influenced by Madonna's frequently changing "look." Girls all over North America copied her fashion style. At first, Madonna wore ripped dancer clothes and tied her hair on top of her head with pieces of mesh. She dyed her hair blonde but let her dark roots show. Later, Madonna dyed her hair platinum blonde. She also helped make underwear popular as outerwear.

▥ Madonna's fashion style could be seen in her movies such as *Desperately Seeking Susan*.

Designer Jeans and Tube Socks

Before the 1980s, most blue jeans looked similar. That was until everyone wanted to wear designer jeans. Designer jeans usually had the designer's name visible on a back pocket. Calvin Klein and Gloria Vanderbilt jeans were very popular. They cost more than blue jeans had in the past, but people were willing to pay for the label. Many types of jeans had zippers all over them, especially zippers that had no purpose. Pinstripes and coloured piping down the sides of the jeans were also trendy.

Jeans and other pants were often worn tucked into baggy tube socks. Many women also wore leg warmers. Leg warmers were originally made to keep dancers' ankles warm.

▨ Denim was in, as long as you could show off the brand names.

TELEVISION

▨ Men copied the style of clothing worn by actor Don Johnson and others in the television show *Miami Vice*. A simple jacket was worn over an often pastel-coloured T-shirt instead of a button-down collar shirt. Don Johnson also made it popular for men to have a partial beard, or stubble. Wearing mesh shoes without socks completed the look.

From Preppie to Grunge

In the early 1980s, the preppie look was all the rage. This fashion trend meant having clean-cut hair for men and women. Men wore pressed pants, while women often wore long, flowing skirts. Preppies liked to wear expensive Ralph Lauren brand clothes. Preppies wore golf shirts in any bright or pastel colour. Not just any golf shirt would do—preppies had to wear Izod shirts, which had small alligators sewn onto the chest. Knit vests were also popular for men. Both men and women wore "deck" or "boat" shoes.

As the decade continued, the

▨ Preppy looks included long strands of fake pearls and cardigan sweaters.

preppie look became less popular. By the end of the decade, the grunge look was coming in. The grunge look was the exact opposite of the preppie look. Sloppy clothes in dull colors, sneakers and messy hair were all part of the grunge fashion that would take over the early part of the 1990s.

Delivered to Canada—the Sikh Refugees

In 1987, a ship dropped off 174 people near the coast of Nova Scotia. These people, all men but one, swam to shore. They were Sikhs who had travelled from a region called Punjab in India.

They hoped to become **refugees** in Canada.

The Indians were illegal immigrants. To become a refugee in Canada, a person must first apply to the government. Refugees must not have committed any crimes and must be able to show that their lives are in danger in their own country. None of these people had applied and few had any identification to prove who they were. Canadian police arrested the Swedish mariner who had delivered the refugees to Canada.

One year earlier, 155 Tamils had been left off the coast of Newfoundland. There was a public outcry against this type of illegal immigration. The Canadian government decided it had to be tougher on the Sikh refugees, since it was the second time this type of immigration occurred. Until they could prove their identity, they were held in Halifax. In the end, most of the Sikhs were allowed to remain in the country.

▪▪ Sikh refugees that were found off the coast of Nova Scotia were bused to Halifax for examinations and questioning.

The Refugee Situation

As immigration became easier, there were more and more people wanting to come to Canada as refugees. Many Canadians debated whether or not we should allow refugees into the country. Some people believed that people falsely claimed to be refugees just to enter the country. Others claimed that Canadians should choose who we let into the country rather than admitting everyone who sought refugee status.

People feared that Canada would become a dumping ground for anyone who wanted to leave his or her own country. The Canadian government decided to change the laws that allowed refugees in. The new laws made it more difficult to enter Canada.

Immigration in the Eighties

During the 1980s, the number of people wanting to move to Canada increased. By the end of the decade, Canada made it easier for certain types of people to immigrate to the country. Immigrants who would add to the country's economy were usually accepted. People from any country who had money to pay for their own start in Canada were encouraged. Skilled workers were also encouraged to come to Canada.

Immigrants to Canada	
1980	143,117
1981	128,618
1982	121,147
1983	89,157
1984	88,239
1985	84,302
1986	99,219
1987	152,098
1988	161,929
1989	192,001

The Boat People

In the late seventies and early eighties, thousands of people from Vietnam came to Canada as refugees. They often travelled on crowded ships through terrible conditions to reach Canada. They came to Canada to escape problems in Vietnam after the war there ended in 1975. In 1979, Canada officially decided to help the boat people. Over the years, Canada allowed tens of thousands of refugees and immigrants from Vietnam to enter the country. Many of the Vietnamese refugees were supported by the Canadian Vietnamese community or by church organizations in Canada. These refugees were given homes and jobs. They were also helped to adjust to Canadian society and the English language. Canada accepted more refugees during this time than many other countries. In 1986, the United Nations honoured Canada for accepting so many refugees.

▓ Many of the Vietnamese refugees fled by boat to Thailand before coming to Canada.

Where Canada's Refugees Come From

From January to August 1987, about 16,900 people applied for refugee status in Canada. Most came from the six countries shown on the map.

Refugees to Canada	
1980	40,638
1981	15,058
1982	17,000
1983	14,062
1984	15,553
1985	17,000
1986	19,485
1987	21,950
1988	27,230
1989	37,361

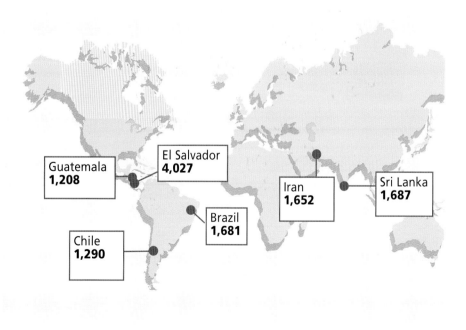

Guatemala
1,208

El Salvador
4,027

Iran
1,652

Sri Lanka
1,687

Brazil
1,681

Chile
1,290

Bryan Adams

From a young age, Bryan Adams had been writing songs and performing. Adams was born in Canada, but spent much of his youth living with his family in other countries, such as England and Portugal. The family settled in Vancouver when Adams was fifteen. Before he was twenty, some of Adams's songs had been recorded by Canadian bands such as Bachman-Turner Overdrive and Prism.

Adams released his first album in 1980. Three years later, his third album, *Cuts Like a Knife*, made him popular around the world. The next album, *Reckless*, became the first Canadian record to sell 1 million copies in Canada. Adams had many other hit songs during the 1980s. He also wrote songs for other singers, including Tina Turner. The Canadian recording industry called him the Artist of the Decade.

▬ The album *Reckless* sold over 8 million copies worldwide.

Tears Are Not Enough

In 1984, an Irish musician named Bob Geldof tried to bring world attention to the people starving to death in Ethiopia, a country in Africa. Geldof gathered together many famous musicians and recorded the song "Do They Know It's Christmas?" All of the money raised from the song went to help the people in Africa. Geldof also

▬ Irish singer Bob Geldof encouraged the music world to get involved with the starvation in Ethiopia. Canadian singers were quick to follow suit with a song to raise money.

arranged a concert, called Live Aid, to raise money.

When Bryan Adams heard about Geldof's work, he decided that Canadians should also help

Sunglasses at Night

Corey Hart, a singer from Montreal, had an international hit with "Sunglasses at Night" in 1983. Corey's good looks and catchy songs won fans all over the world. Over the next few years, Corey had many other hit singles, including "Never Surrender," which won a Juno Award for single of the year. By the age of twenty-four, Corey had sold more than 10 million records worldwide. Many males copied Corey's spiky hairstyle and clothes.

out. He co-wrote a song called "Tears Are Not Enough." The song and video featured many well-known Canadian singers and musicians. The group of musicians called themselves "Northern Lights." Adams also played at the Live Aid concert in the United States.

Loverboy

With their tight leather clothes and energetic music, Loverboy became one of the best-known Canadian rock bands in the early 1980s. The band was formed in Vancouver by two members of the Canadian band *Streetheart* and singer Mike Reno. They released their first album, called *Loverboy*, in 1980. Popular singles such as "The Kid Is Hot Tonight" and "Turn Me Loose" quickly helped the album go gold in Canada. The band was as popular for the members' appearance and music videos as it was for their music.

Loverboy's next album, *Get Lucky,* sold over 500,000 copies as well. By this time, they were already established in Canada. The band was also becoming popular in the United States and Europe. By 1984, Loverboy had sold over 10 million copies of their first three albums.

Loverboy began to lose their popularity by 1987. Although they toured and recorded in 1989 and into the next decade, Loverboy never made it back to the pop charts.

The Nation's Music Station

Although musicians had made videos since the 1960s, it became much more common for musicians to create music videos for their songs during the 1980s. By the end of the decade, nearly

▦ MuchMusic gave Canadian bands a place to be both seen and heard.

every song on the radio had its own video. At first, videos were played on television shows such as *The New Music* out of Toronto. In 1984, MuchMusic became Canada's first twenty-four-hour music video television station. MuchMusic was also based in Toronto. It called itself the "Nation's Music Station," and it played music from across the country. It also played videos by international artists. The "veejays" interviewed musicians and reported on current music news. Two years later, a French language station, MusiquePlus, was started in Montreal.

THE BRITISH INFLUENCE

▦ British pop bands, including groups such as the Police and Duran Duran (pictured here), were particularly popular in Canada during the 1980s. One Canadian band capitalized on the popularity of the British sound. Platinum Blonde was formed by Marc Holmes, an Englishman living in Canada.

Platinum Blonde started as a three-piece band. All members had bleached-blond hair and wore British-inspired clothes. They quickly rose to stardom in Canada after their first album, *Standing in the Dark*, was released in 1984. Platinum Blonde toured with Bryan Adams and Billy Idol. They became famous for their music videos, which were very high-tech for the time. The band was especially popular with young female fans. Thousands of young girls would attend their concerts and scream hysterically.

AIDS

AIDS is a disease that affects the immune system. It first became known in North America in the early 1980s. In the United States, there were many cases of illness that health officials had never seen before. People were frightened of the deadly disease because they did not know what caused it.

The first Canadian AIDS case was discovered in 1978. At that time, the disease was not known or understood. Soon, scientists discovered that AIDS is caused by the HIV virus. They also learned how AIDS was transferred from one person to another. By 1982, the government began to keep track of all of the AIDS cases. Fourteen countries around the world reported cases of AIDS. As of 1988, there were already 1,644 cases of AIDS in Canada. About 30,000 Canadians were infected with the HIV virus.

▦ Quilts were considered a memorial to family and friends who died of AIDS, and they were made across Canada and the United States.

Family Finances

Average families found it difficult to make ends meet. From 1980 to 1989, the income of Canadian families barely changed. The **median income** of families in 1980 was $37,000. In 1989, it was $36,000. In comparison, families made 27 percent more money at the end of the seventies than in 1970. Higher taxes were one of the reasons families made less money in the eighties. In 1980, the average family paid $7,300 in taxes compared to $9,600 in 1989.

▦ In 1989, the percentage of families who were defined as middle-income was 60.8 percent.

Families in Transition

As in the previous two decades, Canadian families consisted of fewer children. The birth rate of Canadians continued to drop steadily. More couples were choosing not to have children at all. Between 1961 and 1981, the number of childless couples nearly doubled to 22 percent. In some cases, couples were just waiting longer to have children.

Birth Rate in Canada (births per 1,000 people)	
1955	28.2
1960	26.8
1965	21.3
1970	17.5
1975	15.8
1980	15.5
1985	14.8

Young Offenders and the Law

In 1984, Canada had a new law called the Young Offenders Act (YOA) to deal with children who broke federal laws. This new law sets out how police and the justice system must treat juvenile offenders between the ages of twelve and eighteen.

All provinces have youth courts to deal with young offenders. If a youth committed a serious crime, such as murder, he or she may be transferred to adult court. The YOA also stated that the names of young offenders could not be made public.

Some people felt that the YOA was not tough enough on young offenders. Even those that committed serious crimes were only sentenced to a few years in juvenile correctional facilities. Many police forces did not like the age limits of the YOA. Older laws had allowed police to deal with child criminals as young as seven years old. Over the next few years, some changes were made to the act to make it tougher on young criminals.

▕▊▊ Dr. Helen Caldicott was the president of Physicians for Social Responsibility in the United States.

Threat of Nuclear War

Both sides of the Cold War rushed to create powerful weapons of destruction during the 1980s. Both the United States and the Soviet Union developed powerful nuclear weapons that could destroy large areas if they were released. Many people were concerned about the possibility of a nuclear war. Some even worried that a war could be started accidentally if the two countries were not careful with their weapons.

In 1983, the National Film Board of Canada made a film called *If You Love This Planet.* The film featured Dr. Helen Caldicott, a scientist. In the film, Dr. Caldicott described what would happen to Earth if one single nuclear bomb exploded. She showed how many people it would kill, and how it would affect people and the environment for decades afterward. The film scared many viewers. It made them take the nuclear arms race more seriously. The United States government criticized *If You Love This Planet,* saying it was **propaganda** and exaggerated the affects of nuclear fallout.

▕▊▊ More and more children were brought up in lone-parent families in the 1980s.

The One-Parent Family

During the 1980s, single parenting became more common. Lone-parent families increased by 34 percent between 1981 to 1991, to nearly 1 million families. By 1991, 17 percent of all Canadian children lived in single-parent homes. Eighty percent of these children lived with their mothers.

The main reason for this increase was the higher rate of divorce. The divorce rate in the mid-1980s was 2.5 out of 1,000 Canadians—five times higher than it had been in the mid-1960s. In 1986, the government passed the Divorce Act, which listed new reasons for which couples could get divorced. By 1987, the divorce rate went up to 3.5 out of 1,000.

More lone-parent families meant that more children lived in poverty. In 1989, 8.5 percent of all children lived in low-income households. Children living only with their mother fared much worse—52.9 percent lived in low-income households.

Control of the Arctic

The land in the northern Arctic belongs to Canada. Canada has had many arguments with the United States over who has control, or sovereignty, of the water in the area. Canada has little power to prevent other countries from entering the area. In 1982, a Law of the Sea Conference ruled that Canada had rights over its Arctic area. Canada claimed that it owned the area called the Northwest Passage. The Northwest Passage is a very important waterway, as it is the shortest route between the United States and Russia. The area is also a wealthy resource for oil, gas, and minerals. The United States did not agree that Canada owned this area.

In 1985, the U.S. sent an **icebreaker**, the *Polar Sea*, through the Northwest Passage without permission from the Canadian government. Many Canadians were angry that the government did not prevent the icebreaker from entering Canadian waters. The Canadian government said it would be more careful about defending its territory.

All across Canada, people protested the testing of cruise missiles over their country.

Cruise Missiles

In the early 1980s, the Canadian government allowed the American government to test cruise missiles over Canada. Cruise missiles are used to carry nuclear weapons. Many Canadians did not agree with the U.S. being allowed to fly these weapons over Canada. They did not want Canada to be a part of the nuclear arms race. Some people felt it would ruin Canada's reputation as a peacekeeping nation.

In 1985, a group of organizations took the Canadian government to court over cruise missiles. They argued that the missiles increased the chances of a nuclear war. The Supreme Court of Canada rejected this argument.

FREE TRADE

In 1986, Canada and the United States worked on an agreement that would allow easier trading of goods and services between the two countries. Already, Canada and the U.S. were important trading partners.

Free trade was supposed to help the economies of both countries. Free trade meant that Canada could sell its resources and other goods to the U.S. market without as many taxes or restrictions. Many Canadians were against free trade with the U.S. They felt that it would mean fewer jobs for Canadians and more dependence on the U.S. With Canada being a smaller market and workforce, many people thought that jobs would go to the United States, where more labour could be found at less cost. Others were anxious to get rid of the taxes and duties paid when goods were brought across the border. The free trade agreement came into effect on January 1, 1989.

Acid Rain

Acid rain became a serious problem for Canada during the 1980s. Acid rain happens when pollution in the air comes to Earth as rain. Canada tried to work out an acid rain agreement with the United States. Much of the acid rain in Canada comes from pollution just south of the border. In 1982, the U.S. refused to set any goals to reduce acid rain. The Americans criticized Canada for making negative films about acid rain. Throughout the decade, the two countries continued to argue about environmental issues.

▭ Pollution from automobiles contributes to acid rain.

WHAT IS ACID RAIN?

▭ Rain falling from the sky usually looks clean and pure. Often, rain can carry invisible pollution. When the pollution makes rain more **acidic**, it becomes acid rain. Acid rain can damage paint and metal. It wears away statues and buildings made of stone. The environment is especially hurt by acid rain. Acid rain changes the balance of the environment. It kills plants and fish and can affect human health.

Shamrock Summit

Canada and the United States have often disagreed about many political topics. In 1985, Prime Minister Mulroney and U.S. President Ronald Reagan held a friendly meeting called the Shamrock Summit. The summit was so named because both men have Irish ancestry.

At the summit, Prime Minister Mulroney and President Reagan agreed on several military defence programs, including the Strategic Defense Initiatives (Star Wars). The two also signed the North American Air Defense Modernization agreement. This agreement updated Canada's DEW (Distant Early Warning) system that protected northern Canada and Alaska from being attacked by other nations.

Another major topic of discussion was free trade between the countries. This meeting eventually led to the free trade agreement.

▭ The Shamrock Summit was held on St. Patrick's Day. Brian and Mila Mulroney played host to Ronald and Nancy Reagan.

Canadian Events of the 1980s

Only one of each of the sets of events happened during the 1980s. The other two happened in other decades. Which are events of the eighties?

1
a) Air India Flight 182 explodes in the air, killing all 329 onboard.
b) Princess Diana dies in an automobile accident in France.
c) Martin Luther King is assassinated.

2
a) *Star Wars* is released to theatres.
b) *Ghostbusters* earns $225 million at the box office.
c) *Due South*, with a Canadian Mountie as its lead character, becomes a popular television show.

3
a) An atomic bomb is dropped on Japan.
b) The nuclear power plant in Chernobyl leaks radioactive waste.
c) A nuclear plant on Three Mile Island is found to cause medical problems for people living in the area.

4
a) Student protesters are killed at a rally at Ohio State University.
b) Many are killed when a bomb explodes in a government building in Oklahoma City.
c) Hundreds of protesters are killed in the Tiananmen Square massacre in China.

5
a) Wayne Gretzky and the Edmonton Oilers win four Stanley Cups.
b) Wayne Gretzky plays his first game in the National Hockey League.
c) Wayne Gretzky retires from professional hockey.

6
a) Canada becomes a nation.
b) Canada celebrates its 100th birthday.
c) Canada gets its own constitution.

7
a) Japanese Canadians are compensated for their treatment by the Canadian government during World War II.
b) Japanese Canadians are removed from their homes and sent to internment camps.
c) Chinese Canadians help to build a railroad across Canada.

8
a) Robert Munsch is born.
b) *The Paper Bag Princess* is published.
c) Robert Munsch creates his own web site.

9
a) Marc Garneau is the first Canadian in space.
b) The seventh Canadian goes into space.
c) The first person walks on the moon.

10
a) The twoonie replaces the two-dollar bill.
b) The loonie replaces the one-dollar bill.
c) Queen Elizabeth's face appears on Canadian money for the first time.

Can you find out when the other events happened?

Answers: 1. a; 2. b; 3. b; 4. c; 5. a; 6. c; 7. a; 8. b; 9. a; 10. b.

True or False

1. The "hosers" were played by John Candy and Dave Thomas.

2. The Rubik's Cube was invented in Canada.

3. Tiananmen Square is a place in China where many people were killed or arrested in 1989.

4. The *Exxon Mediterranean* spilled oil in the Atlantic Ocean.

5. Audrey McLaughlin was the first woman to lead a federal political party in Canada.

Answers:
1. False. Dave Thomas was one of the McKenzie brothers, but the other was played by Rick Moranis, not John Candy.
2. False. The inventor, Erno Rubik, developed the cube in his home country of Hungary.
3. True. The Tiananmen Square massacre happened over a few days in the beginning of June, 1989.
4. False. The *Exxon Valdez*, before it became the *Mediterranean*, spilled the oil off the coast of Alaska.
5. True. Audrey McLaughlin was the leader of the New Democratic party.

Newsmakers

Match the person or people in the news with their story!

1. Best-selling children's book author

2. Lost his gold medal after testing positive for steroids

3. First Canadian man in space

4. Co-wrote and sang "Tears Are Not Enough," a song to help raise money for people starving in Ethiopia

5. Hosted the 1988 Winter Olympics

6. Beat Gordie Howe's record of most points scored

7. One of the McKenzie brothers on *SCTV*

8. Helped create the 1982 Canadian Constitution

9. Wrote the book on which the popular *Anne of Green Gables* movie was based

10. Travelled around the world in a wheelchair

a) Pierre Trudeau
b) Calgary
c) Ben Johnson
d) Marc Garneau
e) Rick Hansen
f) Dave Thomas
g) Lucy Maud Montgomery
h) Bryan Adams
i) Robert Munsch
j) Wayne Gretzky

Answers: 1. i; 2. c; 3. d; 4. h; 5. b; 6. j; 7. f; 8. a; 9. g; 10. e.

CANADA THE 1980s Glossary

acidic: when a substance is not neutral, but measures low on the pH scale

autobiography: a book that a person writes about his or her own life

Cold War: a conflict between two different groups of power; does not involve military action

constitution: the basic principles and laws of a country that determine the powers and duties of the government and guarantee certain rights to the people in it

controversial: causing a public dispute or argument

cyberspace: the Internet or the World Wide Web

deficit: when a government spends more money than it makes

democratic: supporting the view that citizens should elect officials in the government

depression: when the economy of a country is not doing well; unemployment is usually quite high

diplomat: a person who represents his or her country in another country

DNA: an acid that is part of all living things

domestic: within the country

drought: a period of weather with little or no rain

gene: a part of DNA that has specific pieces of information about the living thing from which it came

glasnost: the Russian word meaning "openness;" refers to the new policy of Soviet leader Gorbachev.

icebreaker: a ship designed to break through ice

median income: the amount of money that half of the population earns

mock: make fun of by imitating

NASA (National Aeronautics and Space Administration): the U.S. agency that deals with exploration of outer space

nonfiction: a book that is based on facts rather than made-up stories

propoganda: the spreading of exaggerated opinions or beliefs, passed off as fact

radiation: a form of energy that includes light, heat, and x-rays

referendum: when the citizens of a province or country vote on a certain government decision

refugee: a person who leaves his or her own country to escape danger

rehabilitation: work done to restore a person to good health

satellite: an object, made by people, designed to orbit around Earth, the Moon, or another planet

sovereignty: a political area that is independent of other countries and has its own laws

steroids: drugs that help athletes improve their performance; most competitions do not allow athletes to use these drugs

Tory: another word referring to the Progressive Conservative political party or a member of that party

Learning More

Here are some book resources and Internet links if you want to learn more about the people, places, and events that made headlines during the 1980s.

Books

Christopher, Matt. *On the Ice with—Wayne Gretzky*. New York: Little, Brown, 1997.

Madigan, Carol Orsag. *Test Your 80's Cultural Literacy*. Provo, Utah: ARCO, 1990.

Morton, Desmond. *Shaping a Nation*. Toronto, Ontario: Umbrella Press, 1996.

Rettenmund, Matthew. *Totally Awesome Eighties*. New York: St. Martin's Press, 1996.

Twentieth Century Canada. Calgary, Alberta: Weigl Educational Publishers, 1996.

Internet Links

http://www.schoolnet.ca
SchoolNet contains information about Canada and links to many other web sites on Canadian topics.

http://www.statcan.ca
For current and historical statistics on Canada, check out the Statistics Canada web site.

http://www.cs.cmu.edu/Unofficial/Canadiana/
The Canadian Resource Page provides links to many different government and private web sites on Canadian topics.

To find information about other Canadian subjects, type your key words into a search engine. For example, to get more information about Wayne Gretzky, type his name into a search engine on the Internet. Using Canadian search engines, such as AltaVista Canada (http://www.altavistacanada.com), will often help you find Canadian topics more quickly.